Family Business

THE

Insights Into
Working With Family

by

Michael J. O'Malley, Jr.

with the editorial assistance of

Larry McEnerney

Published in Chicago, Illinois, by Family Business Dynamics,
2102 N. Clifton, Chicago, Illinois 60614.

Design by Muccino Design Group
Illustrations by Harry Briggs

ISBN: 0-9639548-0-6

DEDICATED TO THE NEXT GENERATION...

...AND TO THE MEMORY OF MARY LEYVA

ACKNOWLEDGMENTS

The path I took to take this book from an idea to a reality is one
I did not walk alone. I'd like to thank all of those who walked with me:
*Family, Friends, and especially: Joyce Anderson, James Bone, Gerry Egan,
Stephanie Ferrera, Janet Gill Kennedy, Dom Grassi, Fredda Herz Brown, Roberta LaManna,
Michael Lee, George Martin, Marion McCollom, Rich McGourty, Carol Moran,
Robert Noone, Maggie O'Malley, Peggy O'Malley-Kamibayashi, Ted Rosean,
Ulrich and Ellen Sandmeyer, Sydney Reed, and Marta Vago.*

Special thanks to *Harry Briggs* whose illustrations made
ideas come to life in ways words never could.

It would have been impossible to take even a single step down this path
without the support, talents, and commitment of my two partners:
Alfredo Muccino and *Larry McEnerney*. Thank you for all the gifts you have
given me but most importantly for the gift of your friendships.

The Family Business

The Family & Co. — 2

WORKING WITH FAMILY — 6

KEEPING FAMILY AND BUSINESS HEALTHY — 18

So, You're the Boss — 24

THE BOSS — 28

HIRING FAMILY — 38

FIRING FAMILY — 44

SUCCESSION — 46

You and the Business — 52

TAKING CARE OF NUMERO UNO — 56

WELCOME ABOARD — 68

Parent and Child Corp.   80

    MOM AND DAD   84

    PRIDE AND JOY   98

Husband and Wife Inc.   108

    BEDROOM TO BOARDROOM   112

    THE NEW VOW   120

THE
Family Business

The Family & Co.

Working with family.

It should be so easy, shouldn't it?

After all, these are the same people we love and trust, the people we've sacrificed for, the people who've sacrificed for us, the people we know so well.

To work with them, build a business together — that's a dream come true.

Then why do so many dreams turn out not quite right — or turn out mostly wrong — or turn into nightmares?

Why does it get to be so hard to work with our own families?

Perhaps we don't know our families as well as we thought. We know them as mothers and fathers and sisters and brothers and sons and daughters and husbands and wives and so on.

But we don't know them so well as CEO's and sales reps, as buyers and auditors, as partners and assistants. These are the faces of our families that we see in a family business, and they may not look familiar.

At the heart of so many family business problems is the clash of what we've known — and loved — with what we now come to know. We think: "I can't believe you did that." "I can't believe you said that." "I can't believe you can't do this." "I can't believe you want me to do this."

But this is family, after all, and it's difficult to wish, demand or fire the problems away. And you can't deny that the new realities are not the truth. What you witness is true.

The health of your business and of your relationships with family in the business depends on your ability to recognize, reconcile, and adjust to the new realities. To do this requires insights — insights into the dynamics which shape and govern all family business relationships.

This book offers insights — it will help you understand. We'll look at some hard facts and some unpleasant truths. But we'll look also at strategies that will help you preserve and enhance your relationships with family. After all, working with family is NOT easy.

But it is still a great dream.

Every family business member

feels differently toward the business:

some hate it, some love it; to some

it is a dream come true, to others it

is a nightmare.

E*very family business member sees the business differently. Some see it as a family monument. Some see it as a family gold mine. Some see it as a family mausoleum.*

———»•«———

T*he family business offers something different to every family member: money, power, security, opportunity, shelter, escape.*

———»•«———

W*orking together can first solidify a family — then dissolve it.*

No two family members feel the same way
about the family business.

Good family business relationships do not guarantee business success, but they do guarantee that you can spend more time executing business strategies and less time negotiating family cease-fires.

"Now that we're working together,
we'll get along better."

FAMOUS WATER COOLER · CONVERSATIONS

BLAH, BLAH, BLAH
BLAH, BLAH—

"Oh, I don't need a contract. He's my uncle."

"...Of course she'll get a raise. She's <u>darling</u> daughter!"

"You're his son — you tell him we missed quota!"

There is no family business member — alive or dead —
who ever believed he received the recognition and accolades
he deserved.

———◆———

The BEST thing about working in a family business is
working with your family.

———◆———

The WORST thing about working in a family business is
working with your family.

Family members assume everything and discuss nothing.

Some of the things that family business members assume:
- *Spouses assume they will not be treated like employees.*
- *Children assume that parents will "look the other way" at least once.*
- *In-laws assume that they have a job for life.*

The most successful family businesses make more written agreements than oral agreements.

S*ome of the advantages of working with your family:*

- *a shared passion*
- *a lifetime of communicating*
- *a history of trust*

———

S*ome of the disadvantages of working with your family:*

- *a clash of passions*
- *a lifetime of not communicating*
- *a history of distrust*

Some times are better than others for discussing family business.

F*amily members usually underestimate the degree to which some in the family are emotionally ATTACHED to the business.*

F*amily members usually underestimate the degree to which some in the family are emotionally DETACHED from the business.*

The family business is an equal opportunity employer for the whole family.

N*o family business member — alive or dead — is glad she said, "That's OK, you're family, you can take care of that later."*

———

F*or many family business members the business is the focal point of their lives. It is more important than their spouses, their children, or their friends.*

Family business can occasionally make a poor relationship good and a good relationship great.

Family business can frequently make a good relationship bad and a bad relationship terrible.

MYTH 3

You can keep family issues separate from family business issues.

Join family business groups.

Attend workshops and seminars that

cover family business issues.

Do not make the family a slave to the business.

———•◦•———

Remember to celebrate that the family is in business together.

———•◦•———

Set aside 1% of the business profits each year in a Family Business Celebration Fund. Use the fund to celebrate:
- *the anniversary of the founding of the business*
- *the addition of a new family member to the business*
- *the sale of the business.*

Family members not in the business often feel entitled
to information about the business.

Keep a written and oral history of the family business.

———◦———

After you have compiled the family business history, use the Family Celebration Fund to throw a party. Give family, friends, and employees a copy of the history.

———◦———

Establish a family business council.

Invite family business professionals to speak at your family council meetings. Among the topics:

- *succession planning*
- *entering the family business*
- *the impact of death and illness on the business*

———⇥∘⇤———

Establish an outside board.

———⇥∘⇤———

If your aim with your outside board is to increase objectivity and decrease emotions then DO NOT include family members.

It's easy to find a solution to a
bad family business relationship. It's hard
to make the solution work.

But it's your family. Try seven
times seven times to make it work.
Then seven times seven more.

Never give up.

So,
You're
the Boss

Being the boss in any business is challenging, but it's even more so in a family business. Every decision the boss in the family business makes is rigorously examined by three powerful and divergent groups:

- Non-family business members

- Family business members

- The rest of the family

Each group has different bench marks for evaluating the boss's decisions. What is considered fair to one group is considered nepotism to another.

"Something that should have been done years ago" according to non-family business members can be an outrage to a family member not in the business: "You can't fire him — he's my son, he's your brother!"

Considering the task that all family business bosses face — to meet the demands of business while functioning as someone's aunt or uncle, husband or wife, mother or father, brother or sister — it is no wonder that they feel underpaid.

Being a good boss has nothing to

do with being a good spouse, parent,

in-law, aunt or uncle. Unfortunately,

all the family members who work for

you will think that it does.

N*ever demand more of a family business member than you demand of a non-family business member.*

———

T*o the family member who works for you, a business promise you cannot keep is a family promise you didn't keep.*

———

R*emember that there is no such thing as a secret in a family business.*

Give family members a chance to step out of your shadow.

As soon as you make an exception for one family business member, you may as well tell all the others.

———

What they say: "I want to be treated just like every other employee."

———

What they mean: "I won't object to some special treatment now and then."

The expectations that family business members have of you will be unreasonably high. You might as well tell them up front that they will be disappointed.

———⇒•⇐———

No matter how hard you try to treat every family business member fairly, someone will feel mistreated.

———⇒•⇐———

If you want family business members to resent you, make sure to withhold business information they feel entitled to.

It is inevitable that in the eyes
of at least one family business member,
you will fall from grace.

"*Of course I'm wrong. I'm always wrong.
I've been wrong since we were kids.*"

"*45 years old and she still calls me Donnie!*"

"*Of course it's not enough. It's never been enough.*"

No one promotes your family business better than your family.

————⊷⊶————

When the members of the work pool have gone, the members of the gene pool will still be there.

"I don't care what others in the family think."

First and foremost, family business members want to be recognized by you for their contributions to the business.

⎯⎯⎯⎯

After recognition, every family business member will want something different: maybe money, maybe power, maybe time, maybe your job.

⎯⎯⎯⎯

When you create a business role for a family member where there is none, you have planted the seeds for a problem that did not need to exist.

What you need for the business will often conflict with what family members want you to do for them.

———⊶◦⊷———

It is virtually impossible to compensate family members fairly.
- *No amount may be enough to reward their passion and commitment.*
- *Any amount may be too much if they don't contribute to the business.*

———⊶◦⊷———

Make an exception for a family business member only if you are willing to make that same exception for a non-family business member.

When you think of hiring a family

member, remember this:

All of your objective brain cells are

out to lunch.

If it was difficult to say:

    NO, you can't have a new bike,

Then think of what it will be like to say:

- *NO, you can't have a raise.*
- *NO, you can't be the president.*
- *NO, you can't have the business.*

Three noble — *but wrong* — reasons for hiring a family member:

- *"She's such a good person."*
- *"It will only be for a short time."*
- *"He needs my help."*

Don't set them up for failure.

Considering hiring a family member?
Can you say: "He is qualified to meet
a need we have in the business?"
Can't say it?
Then don't hire him.

———◆———

Hired him anyway?
Do yourself and him a favor.
Give him five hours of company time a week to find
another job.
Yes, pay him; it's a great investment.

Before being allowed to join the family firm, family members should have at least 3 years of outside work experience.

First and foremost, family members join the business because they love the idea of working with family.

———⇒◦⇐———

Family members join a family firm because they trust the family. They leave when they feel that their trust has been betrayed.

———⇒◦⇐———

Listen when a family member tells you what she wants from the business. See if you can match what she wants with what the business needs.

"By the way — I fired our son today."

Three good reasons for firing family members:

- *They have failed to fulfill their roles and responsibilities to the business.*
- *They have failed to fulfill their roles and responsibilities to the business.*
- *They have failed to fulfill their roles and responsibilities to the business.*

Begin succession planning the day

after the first family member joins

the business.

Founders wish to pass on the family business for three reasons:

- *to provide security for future generations*
- *to leave a legacy*
- *to bind the family together.*

———◈———

Remember:

- *you can't protect them from everything*
- *memories fade*
- *family members can't be bound to each other, they can only embrace each other.*

"Dad, I'd like to talk with you about your succession plans."

Why family business owners don't develop succession plans:

1. You have to tell one child you are leaving the business to another.
2. The child who takes over will probably fail miserably.
3. The child who takes over will probably succeed brilliantly.
4. Planning the succession for your business feels like planning the eulogies for your funeral.
   Only not as much fun.

Succession Planning

Rarely do family business founders feel that the next generation gives them the recognition they deserve.

———

Put as much energy into preparing the business for the next generation as you did in building it for this one.

———

To guarantee that your legacy will be short-lived, make sure to leave succession planning in the hands of the next generation.

You
and the
Business

The family business can be a place of tremendous freedom or it can be a prison. It can provide unparalleled opportunities or it can snuff out even the smallest flicker of individuality. It can provide a wonderful way of life or no life at all.

Will it be a bit of heaven or a bit of hell?

What the business will be for you is NOT a mystery. Right there, right in front of you — if you choose to look — are the clues which can show you your future.

The first clue is found in your answer to this question: how do you serve your family? Are you a caretaker, a jester, a peacemaker, or perhaps the valve through which the family releases all of its steam? When you work with family in business they will expect that you serve them in the same manner. More than likely you will deliver. Out of habit you will sing the same song you've sung a thousand times before.

The second clue is even more telling: Why are you in the business? Do you owe it to your family? Do you believe it is your destiny? Do you have a choice? Or are you there because you love it, you want to be part of it? Your motives determine if it is passion and commitment you bring to the business, or resentment and frustration.

The clues are easy to find — and even easier to ignore. Family members want to believe that family business is virgin territory; a place where histories are forgotten. They are wrong. A family business is just a different backdrop, the stage and the actors are the same. It's up to you to take control of the script.

The demands of business and the

demands of family can be suffocating.

Never stop breathing.

If it was difficult to grow and develop in the family, it will be impossible to do so in the family business.

If you fail to say what you want, then the family business will fail to get what it needs.

> The family business is always a safe, warm and friendly place.

Don't try to fill someone else's shoes, just your own.

F*ace the realities of your life in the family business:*
- *If you are unhappy, then you are unhappy.*
- *If your contributions are not being recognized, then they are not being recognized.*
- *If you believe that you have made a mistake by working there, then you've made a mistake.*

——▸•◂——

A*fter you admit the reality, do something about it.*
GET ON WITH IT! Don't wait for divine intervention.

Never work for another family member because you believe you owe him. Pay the debt some other way—any other way.

———————————

Never hire another family member because you believe you owe him. Pay the debt some other way—any other way.

The strategies that will help you manage tension in the family can be useless in helping you manage tension in the family business.

Spend *five minutes of every business day speaking with family business members about something other than business. Need suggestions?*

- *Whatever happened to Gary Hart?*
- *How's your cat?*
- *Seen any good movies?*

———◆———

Accept *other family business members for who they are. Stop wishing, hoping, or demanding that they become someone else.*

O*nce — to do a favor — you can work for another family member for free. Only once.*

———⊶•⊷———

N*EVER yell at, dress down, or humiliate a family business member in front of others.*

You shouldn't say, "I love you," at work.

NEVER, ever, agree to speak with one family member on behalf of another. Fight, with all your strength, against the pull to get sucked into the middle. You will not do anyone, including yourself, an ounce of good.

———⟫•⟪———

If you are involved in a conflict with another family business member, ask yourself:

- What part did I play in starting this conflict?
- What part do I play in prolonging it?

N_{EVER} *confuse spending time at the family business with spending time with the family. They are not the same thing. Not even close.*

Y_{ou} *can't change how you were treated in your family but you can influence how you will be treated in the family business.*

$D_{on't}$ *use problems in your business as an excuse to avoid problems in your life.*

The only thing you can change in a family business relationship is you. To wait for someone else to change is to wait for death and taxes to be abolished.

———◆———

If you have reached a business agreement with another family business member, but it is not in writing, then you have agreed that in the future you will disagree.

Join the family business because you want to prove something to yourself, not because you want to prove yourself to someone else.

The role you play in your family is often the one you will be expected to play in the family business.

———◦———

Know what the business "gives" you. Try to determine what it gives other family members.

———◦———

If your vision of your role has changed, DON'T KEEP IT A SECRET — TELL THE BOSS.

I*f you are joining a family business and you believe any of the following:*

- *in a family business it's all for one and one for all*
- *in a family business, there's less pressure*
- *in a family business you get special treatment —*

then immediately send your résumé to General Motors.

I*f you have ever said:*
"Someday this will all be mine" —
then immediately send your résumé to General Motors.

FAMOUS WATER COOLER · CONVERSATIONS

BLAH, BLAH, BLAH BLAH, BLAH—

"Your roles and responsibilities in the business will be..."

"My expectations for you in the business are..."

"My vision for the firm and the part you will play in making that vision work is..."

Before setting foot inside the door of the family business, know what your personal, non-negotiable boundaries are.

———

Before entering the family business, you need to have developed the virtue of unconditional forgiveness.

———

Your home may be your castle but the family business is not your fiefdom.

If you don't like the relationship you have with another family member outside of the business, you will loathe it inside the business.

—————◆—————

Do not join the family firm unless you have given some thought to how the demands of business might undermine your relationships with other family members.

7

"Don't hold back — I welcome criticism."

Joining the family business is like getting married. It never solves anything.

There are thousands of unspoken rules and values in a family business. Learn what they are.

Here are some common ones:

- *Say what you want as long as it is what I want to hear.*
- *When you separate from your spouse, you separate from the business.*
- *Speak your mind, but mind what you speak.*
- *No one gets theirs until the boss gets his.*

I*f you* are replacing someone in the firm who was fired, find out the reasons for their firing.

———◆———

D*o not* accept any job in the firm unless your roles and responsibilities are clearly defined in writing.

———◆———

D*o not* accept any job in the firm where your salary is less than someone else's in a comparable position.

In a family business your weaknesses
are magnified and your strengths are
taken for granted.

Parent
and
Child Corp.

66 We walked hand in hand. Nothing could come between us. Not the time I quit Boy Scouts without telling him; or when I totaled the car; or when he discovered that my roommate in college was a she rather than a he. I know at those times he felt disappointed, angry, and concerned, but he never took his hand from mine. In fact, it always seemed he would squeeze a little tighter.

"Hand in hand we walked into his business together. He was proud and confident. I never saw him happier. 'Look around you,' he said, 'this is mine. I built it. Someday I want it to be yours.'

"I wanted it, but more importantly I wanted to keep feeling his hand holding mine. I wanted to stay with him; it was safe and I felt strong. Being with him would allow me, as it always had, to jump without risking a fall; invest without suffering a loss; test myself without the fear of failing.

"But after a time his grip became vise-like and my hand began to hurt. I wanted to be free from his grasp. I wanted to feel for myself what it felt like to fall, lose, and fail.

"He would say, 'Go ahead, do what you need to do — but you won't do it here.' He let go of my hand. I left and I did OK, but I never allowed myself to fall very far, invest too much or take very difficult tests. I couldn't. I never had the confidence that I had when I was with him. Without my hand in his, I felt too scared.

"Strangers now own his business — and my daughter works in mine. I try not to squeeze her hand very hard, but I know I do. I can't help it. I can't bear the thought of her falling, losing, and failing."

If you enjoyed watching your children

grow in the family, you will love

watching them grow in the business.

To guarantee that at least one of your children will resent you forever, make sure to pit them against each other in the family business.

———⇥•⇤———

Bring your children into the family firm because of the value they will bring to the business, not because of the value they bring to the family.

It is very difficult to assess your child's strengths and weaknesses objectively.

When it comes to your child's performance in the business, trust a non-family business member's judgment more than your own. Much more.

MYTH
8

"I don't care what happens to the business,
I just want the kids to be happy."

Hire your child only if...
- she is qualified to fill the position.
- she wants the job.
- you would hire her if she wasn't your offspring.
- after firing her you will still be on speaking terms.

———

Contrary to what you may hope and believe, you are not the ideal business mentor for your child.

"*Someday, son, it will all be yours.*"

"*Listen — don't let this go any further...*"

"*Don't worry, we can sign that later!*"

Your child will always fall short in appreciating your sacrifices and contributions to the business.

———

Heard in the kitchen:
"That's between you and your son. I'm staying out of it!"

———

Take part in your child's business performance appraisal only if he reports directly to you.

Children in family businesses often feel that they are
under intense scrutiny.

If at work you cannot tell your child:

- *I made a mistake —*
- *I'm sorry —*
- *I was wrong —*
- *I love you —*

then DO NOT hire him.

———⟫•⟪———

Every child in a family business needs a non-family mentor.

———⟫•⟪———

Your children's business roles and responsibilities should meet the needs of the family firm, not your needs or theirs.

Some needs that parents have:

- *to have a successor*
- *to make up for a past wrong*
- *to show their children they love them*
- *to be taken care of*
- *to show off and be confirmed.*

———⟫•⟪———

Some needs that children have:

- *to be successors*
- *to make up for past wrongs*
- *to show their parents they love them*
- *to be taken care of*
- *to show off and be confirmed.*

Heard in the bedroom:
"I can't believe he's in charge of our accounting.
Wasn't it just yesterday that he got a D in algebra?"

Your children do not all have the same set of skills
and capabilities.

"I'll be retiring in a few months."

"Please Mom, I beg you, tell Dad I lost the account."

Some of the advantages of working with your child:
- *save money on character reference checks*
- *less likely to sue you for all of your money*
- *can save on club membership entry fees.*

———⟫•⟪———

Some of the disadvantages of working with your child:
- *character references may be unreliable*
- *could sue you for at least some of your money*
- *will still sign your club membership number.*

On your child's first day on the job, introduce him or her to the other members of the family firm. Do not make it a secret.

———

The family business is not a prize. Do not make your children compete for it.

———

Heard in the car:
"Why are you always criticizing him?"
"Why are you always defending him?"

Is there anything more satisfying
than having your child say,
"I want to work with you here, by your side?"

When you work with your parents you will see sides of them which you have never seen before.

Parents may hear your ideas for the business better from someone other than yourself.

―――――――

You will have to learn how to wait. You will get yours only after your parents have gotten theirs.

―――――――

Forget trying to get your parents to see it your way. Instead, try to see it their way.

Parents assume and expect that the relationship pattern that exists in the family will be the same one that will exist in the family business.

———

Do NOT work with your parents until you:
- are living on your own.
- owe them less than $1000.
- can say "No, I can't make it to dinner this Sunday."

Do not expect or demand that your parents take care of you in the business.

When you work with your parents you may discover the following:

- *They are not perfect. They are human.*
- *They are more flexible than you thought.*
- *They are tougher than you thought.*

Your title may read: Chairman, President or CEO, but your parents still see you as Son or Daughter.

Son, any time you want to speak with me, I'm available.

Y*ou have no chance of winning a business argument with your parents if all you have is your opinion against theirs.*

I*f, however, you can refer to evidence which supports your argument, you now have a 49% chance of winning the argument.*

"I have to work here, I had no choice."

Every parent has expectations for his child in the business. It is the child's job to find out what those expectations are.

———⸗•⸲———

If you discover what those expectations are, you will have discovered how to build a work relationship which is meaningful and valuable.

3 *GREAT Reasons NOT TO work with your parents:*

   1. It would give my relationship with my parents a new start.

   2. They need me.

   3. I owe them.

———➤•◀———

3 *GREAT reasons TO work with your parents:*

   1. I love the business. I want to be a part of it.

   2. I love the business. I want to be a part of it.

   3. I love the business. I want to be a part of it.

Y*ou may think you deserve the business, but your parents may think you haven't earned it.*

———◆———

N*ever underestimate the deep sense of possessiveness your parents have toward their business.*

———◆———

P*arents have dreams and visions too. Your becoming successful in the business may not be one of them.*

Parents feel tremendous pride and satisfaction
when their child joins them in business.
For many, it is the ultimate tribute.
Let your parents relish the moment.
Let them show you off. Let them celebrate.

Husband
and
Wife Inc.

Mike take you Cathy to be my lawfully wedded wife.

I Mike take you Cathy to be my business partner (we don't need a contract).

To have and to hold, in sickness and in health.

To open and close the store, during markdown sales and markup prices.

All the years of our lives.

All the fiscal year closings of our lives."

Most men and women, individually and as couples, get married only after thinking long and hard. They deliberate — sometimes forever — about the changes marriage will bring: in careers, lifestyles, friendships, families. And then, after all the musing and compromising and preparing, they make their commitment.

Most men and women, individually and as couples, begin working together after little or no thought. They don't deliberate — even for a moment — about the changes working together will bring: in their quality of life, their children, their marriage.

And so, without musing or compromising or preparing, they walk into work. Without the tools they need for success they commit themselves to a journey which puts at risk all they have built and all they dream of building.

Tough business decisions are always

lonely but they are less lonely when

they are made with your spouse.

Some of the advantages of working with your spouse:

- *Every meal you eat out is tax deductible.*
- *When your kids have an emergency they only need to make one phone call.*
- *You can always get a ride to work.*

Some of the disadvantages of working with your spouse:

- *You have no one to complain to at home.*
- *Your home-cooked meals tend to be prepared by people like Sara Lee and Mr. Micro Chef.*
- *You spend too many Friday nights watching Wall Street Week.*

M*any people feel* **MORE** *freedom when they are working with a spouse. More freedom to be themselves and to take chances.*

M*any people feel* **LESS** *freedom when they are working with a spouse. Less freedom to be themselves and to take chances.*

People marry because they are in love.
It's an awful reason to work together.

Most marriage relations are characterized by
EMOTIONAL ATTACHMENT.

———◦———

Most business relations are characterized by
EMOTIONAL DETACHMENT.

———◦———

You marry someone you love, but you hire
someone who's good for business.

Put as much thought into choosing your spouse as a partner in business as you did in choosing him or her as a partner in life. (Maybe more.)

———

The things you love about your spouse may be the things that drive you crazy in a business partner.

———

Remember: you put your name on a wedding certificate, not on a 5-year business plan.

If you view working with your spouse
as an opportunity to spend more time together,
to find out what she or he does all day, or
to put some life back into your marriage —

then don't even THINK about working together.

Building a life together is not

the same thing as building a

business together.

Your work relationship will go through the same periods
that your personal relationship has gone through:
infatuation, courting, engagement, cold feet, marriage,
honeymoon, "What have we done!"

It's impossible to predict if working with your spouse
will cause your relationship to be stronger or weaker, richer
or poorer, better or worse. But you can predict — with
100% certainty — that working together will change your
relationship forever.

Working together may produce results entirely different than what you had hoped. Rather than more intimacy in your relationship, you may end up with more distance; rather than getting more attention, you may be more neglected.

———

At home, your spouse may make meeting your needs a priority. At work, your needs may not even make the "To Do" list.

When you work with your spouse, all the things you love about them will still be there.

Some days, however, they may be harder to see.

Working together is not a test.

*he demands you can make of your spouse at home are not
e same demands you can make at work.*

---

*on't look for your business partnership to fill a hole in
ur relationship. It is likely just to make the hole bigger.*

11

"You want it in writing? Oh — you must not love me!"

Use the blueprints from your existing relationship to build
a foundation for your business relationship.

M*ake it a policy to do things together which are unrelated to the business.*

—————»·•·«—————

A*t work, do not demand or expect time to deal with relationship problems — it is neither the time nor the place.*

—————»·•·«—————

D*o not measure how strong or weak your marriage is by how your spouse treats you at work.*

THE
Family Business

Dear Reader,

Each family member's experience in working with family is different. If you would
like to share your insights, observations, and experiences, please write them down,
with your name, address, phone number, your family business, and what generation
you represent in the family firm. Please mail this information to:

Michael J. O'Malley, Jr.
2102 N. Clifton
Chicago, IL 60614
Tel. 312.477.0247
Fax 312.477.0248

I would like to share your wisdom with other family members in a future book.
Thank You.